What Makes Me Beautiful?

Soul Vision Works Publishing
P.O.Box 360063
Brooklyn, New York 11236
www.soulvisionworks.com

We dedicate this book to Edna Victoria Jacobs, whose life on earth exemplified the principles in this book.

Library of Congress Cataloging-in Publication Data

Vision, David, 1957-
   What Makes Me Beautiful? / written by David & Mutiya Vision ; illustrated by Ignacio Alcantara.
      p. cm.
   Summary: Children are told that their character and personal values make them beautiful.
   ISBN 0-9659538-4-X
   [1. Beauty, Personal--Fiction. 2. Character--Fiction.] I. Vision, Mutiya Sahar, 1969- II.
Alcantara, Ignacio, ill. III. Title.

PZ7. V8227Who 2004
[E]--dc22

2004059160

Manufactured in China

What Makes Me Beautiful?

Written By David & Mutiya Vision

Illustrated by Ignacio Alcantara

Soul Vision Works Publishing   New York

Mom says I'm beautiful because
I'm **thoughtful.**
I think of ways to make others happy!

*Dad says I'm beautiful because I'm **smart**. I love to ask questions and learn new things!*

*Grandma thinks I'm beautiful because I'm **generous**.*
I share the things I have with others!

*Auntie thinks I'm beautiful because I'm **clever**.*
I'm always thinking of ways to make
things around me better.

*Grandpa thinks I'm beautiful because
I'm **helpful**.
I help others without being told.*

My sister thinks I'm beautiful because
*I'm **fun** to be with.*
I make others smile and feel good.

My cousin thinks I'm beautiful because
*I'm **creative.***
I love making up new games we can play.

*My friends think I'm beautiful because I'm **reliable** and **work well with others.** If I say I will do something, I make sure it gets done.*

My Uncle thinks I'm beautiful because
I'm **honest**.
I always tell the truth.
I mean what I say and say what I mean.

Most of all, I know I'm beautiful because
of all the things I do and say.
I help people, and places I encounter
become more beautiful too!

*What are some things you do
that make **you** beautiful?*

If you enjoyed reading this book, you'll want to add other
Soul Vision Works books to your special collection.
Look out for these titles:

**Daddy Loves His Baby Girl
The Sister Who Copied Me
Missing You
Only You Can Make You Happy
My Very Breast Friend
Disabilities
If Only I Could
Adapt
Who's That Crying?
Practice Makes Perfect
Isn't There anything Here With A Yes On It?**

Get all these and much, much more on the web at:
www.soulvisionworks.com

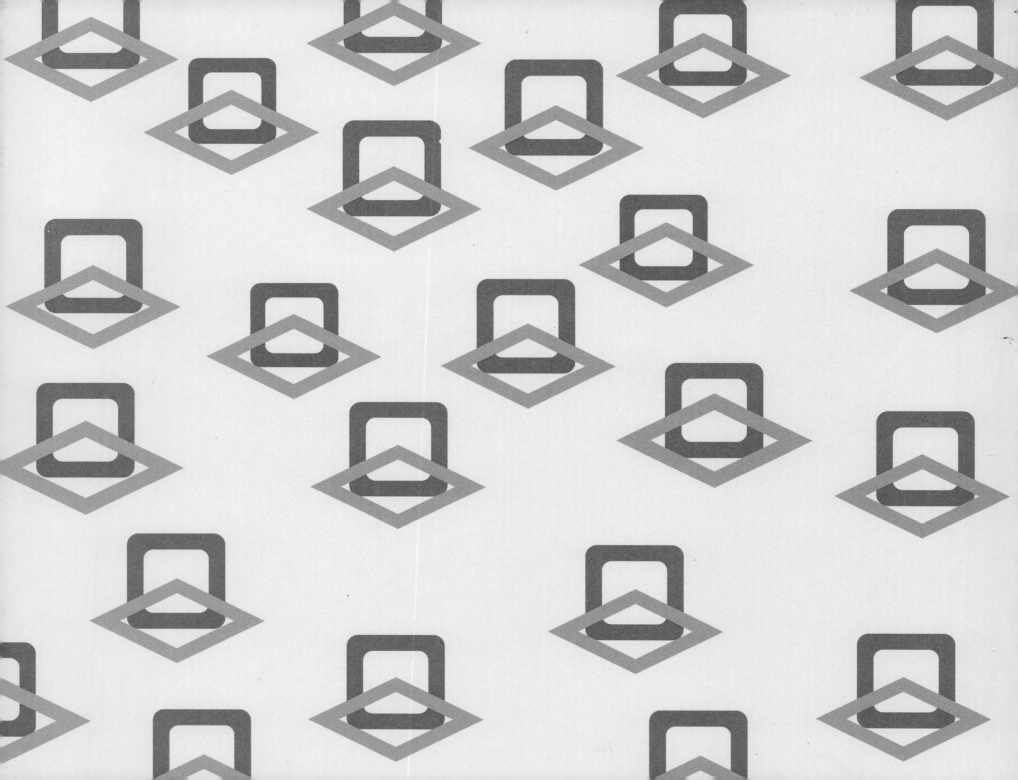